Advanced

THREE EPISODES

for Trumpet and Piano

James Curnow

CURNOW MUSIC

EXCLUSIVELY DISTRIBUTED BY

HAL•LEONARD CORPORATION
7777 W. BLUEMOUND RD. P.O. BOX 13819 MILWAUKEE, WI 53213

Edition Number: CMP 0978-05

Three Episodes
for Trumpet and Piano
James Curnow

ISBN 90-431-2327-7

James Curnow

James Curnow was born in Port Huron, Michigan and raised in Royal Oak, Michigan. He lives in Nicholasville, Kentucky where he is president, composer, and educational consultant for Curnow Music Press, Inc. of Lexington, Kentucky, publishers of significant music for concert band and brass band. He also serves as Composer-in-residence (Emeritus) on the faculty of Asbury College in Wilmore, Kentucky, and is editor of all music publications for The Salvation Army in Atlanta, Georgia.

His formal training was received at Wayne State University (Detroit, Michigan) and at Michigan State University (East Lansing, Michigan), where he was a euphonium student of Leonard alcone, and a conducting student of Dr. Harry Begian. His studies in composition and arranging were with F. Maxwell Wood, James Gibb, Jere Hutchinson, and Irwin Fischer.

James Curnow has taught in all areas of instrumental music, both in the public schools (five years), and on the college and university level (twenty-six years). He is a member of several professional organizations, including the American Bandmasters Association, College Band Directors National Association, World Association of Symphonic Bands and Wind Ensembles and the American Society of Composers, Authors and Publishers (ASCAP). In 1980 he received the National Band Association's Citation of Excellence. In 1985, while a tenured Associate Professor at the University of Illinois, Champaign-Urbana, Mr. Curnow was honored as an outstanding faculty member. Among his most recent honors are inclusion in Who's Who in America, Who's Who in the South and Southwest, and Composer of the Year (1997) by the Kentucky Music Teachers Association and the National Music Teachers Association. He has received annual ASCAP standard awards since 1979.

As a conductor, composer and clinician, Curnow has traveled throughout the United States, Canada, Australia, Japan and Europe where his music has received wide acclaim. He has won several awards for band compositions including the ASBDA/Volkwein Composition Award in 1977 (Symphonic Triptych) and 1979 (Collage for Band), the ABA/Ostwald Award in 1980 (Mutanza) and 1984 (Symphonic Variants for Euphonium and Band), the 1985 Sixth International Competition of Original Compositions for Band (Australian Variants Suite), and the 1994 Coup de Vents Composition Competition of Le Havre, France (Lochinvar).

Curnow has been commissioned to write over two hundred works for concert band, brass band, orchestra, choir and various vocal and instrumental ensembles. His published works now number well over four hundred. His most recent commissions include the Tokyo Symphony Orchestra (Symphonic Variants for Euphonium and Orchestra), the United States Army Band (Pershing's Own, Washington, D.C.-Lochinvar, Symphonic Poem for Winds and Percussion), Roger Behrend and the DEG Music Products, Inc. and Willson Band Instrument Companies (Concerto for Euphonium and Orchestra), the Olympic Fanfare and Theme for the Olympic Flag (Atlanta Committee for the Olympic Games, 1996), the Kentucky Music Teachers Association/National Music Teachers Association in 1997 (On Poems of John Keats for String Quartet) and Michigan State University Bands (John Whitwell, Director of Bands) in honor of David Catron's twenty-six years of service to the university and the university bands (Ode And Epinicion).

THREE EPISODES
For Trumpet and Piano

James Curnow (ASCAP)

Allegro con moto
Largo moderato e espressivo
Cadenza: Allegro energico

Approximate duration: 7:30

Second place winner of the I.T.G. 200 composition competition, and
Commissioned for and first performed by Edward Bach, trumpet, and Arthur
Tollefson, piano, and the Focus on Piano Literature, School of Music,
The University of North Carolina at Greensboro, June 8, 2000.

Program Note

Three Episodes for Trumpet and Piano is a diverse three-movement work (fast, slow, fast), seven and one-half minutes in duration, designed to capture the entire range of expressive and technical aspects of both instruments. Set in a neoclassical style, this work features the interplay of all melodic, motivic, harmonic and rhythmic material, equally distributed between both performers.

An episode is one of a series of related events. *Three Episodes* is one of many commissioned works, being performed in a series of concerts that celebrate the 11th anniversary of Focus on Piano Literature and the opening of a new Music Building.

Movement 1 – *Allegro con moto*

Set in a modified Sonata-Allegro form, this movement is melodically based on the material first presented in the piano as an energetic fanfare, and immediately imitated by the soloist. After a few measures of developmental material, the first theme is transformed into a melodically related second theme. This theme is an extremely lyrical and expressive melody first stated by the soloist and reiterated by the pianist. Following a brief development of motivic material taken from both themes, the recapitulation restates the opening fanfare theme a fifth lower than first presented. The concluding measures feature the pianist stating the fanfare while the soloist plays accented repetitive figures.

Movement 2 – *Largo moderato e espressivo*

This movement focuses on the expressive qualities of both performers. The form is basically theme and variation, where the variations are based mostly on motifs extracted from the primary theme, rather than the theme itself. The underpinning for this movement is the continuous reiteration of the rhythmic ostinato, which begins the movement and gradually develops throughout, until it reaches its quiet and subtle conclusion.

Movement 3 – *Cadenza (Senza misura): Allegro energico*

After the presentation of an exclamatory fanfare-like cadenza, this final movement features a spirited five-part rondo (ABACA) that exudes excitement and energy. The movement concludes with the soloist playing the opening cadenza, juxtaposed over motivic excerpts from the A theme in the piano.

Commissioned for and first performed by Edward Bach, Trumpet, and Arthur Tollefson, Piano, at the Focus on Piano Literature, School of Music, The University of North Carolina at Greensboro, June 8 , 2000, and Second Place Winner of the 2001 International Trumpet Guild Composition Competition.

THREE EPISODES

for Trumpet and Piano

James Curnow (ASCAP)

1.

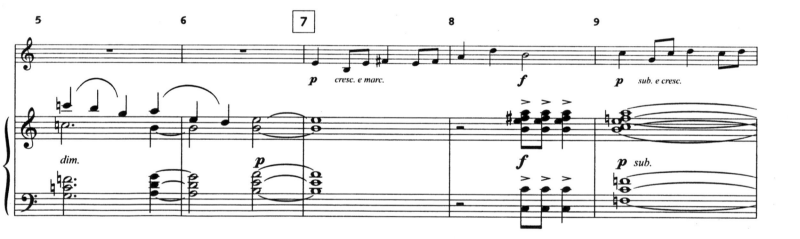

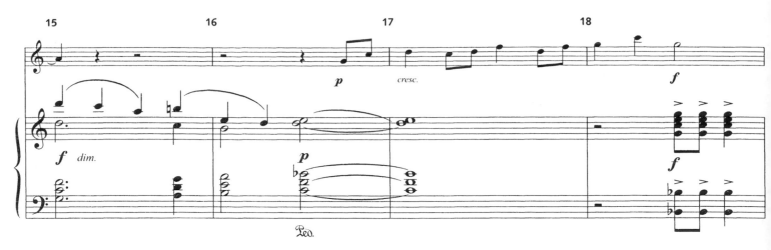

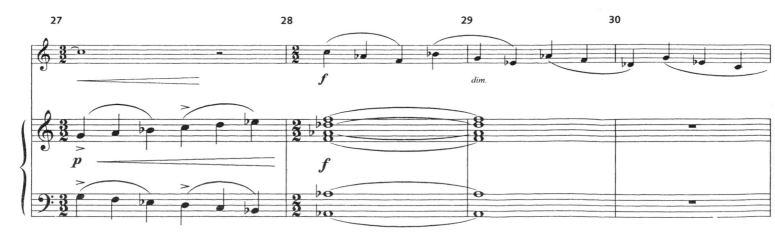

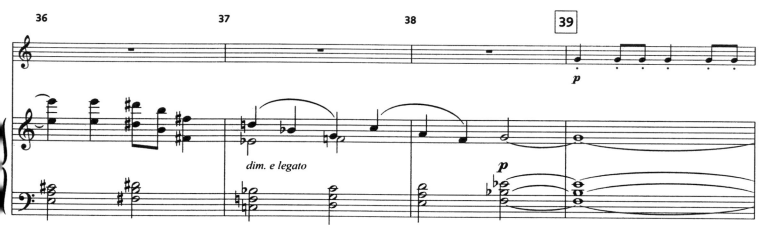

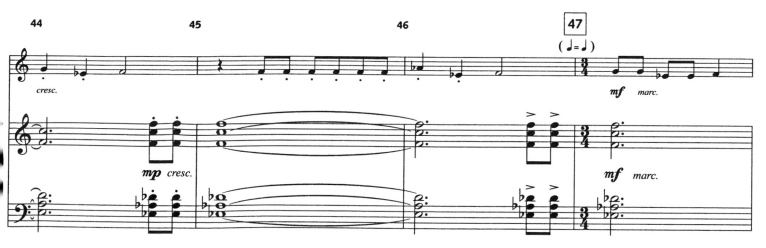

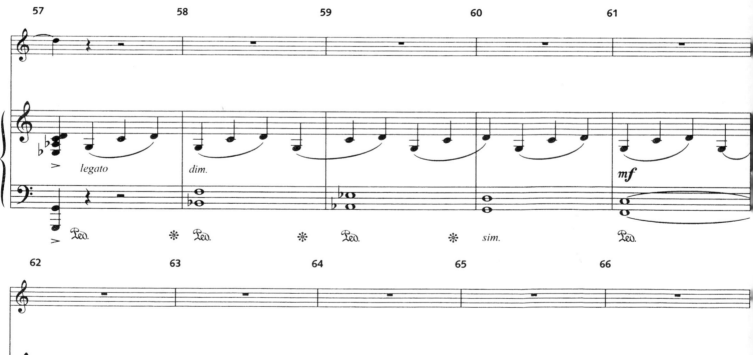

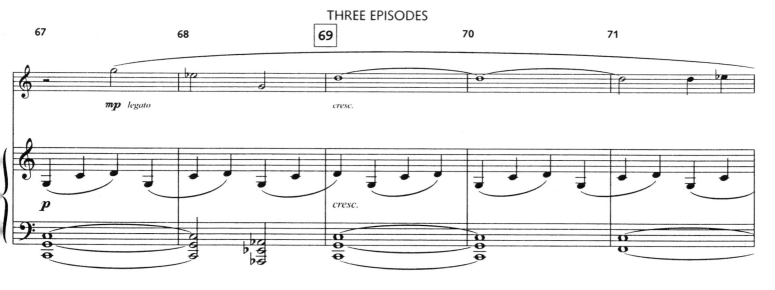

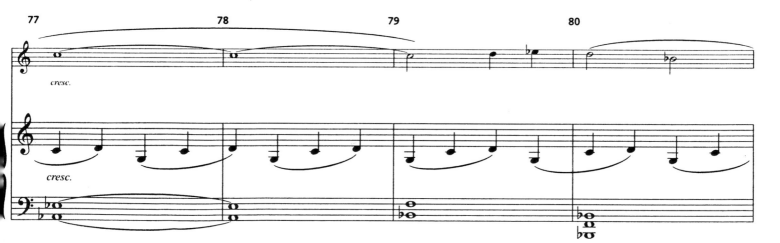

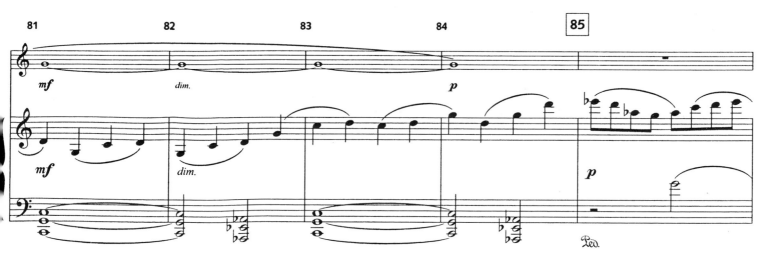

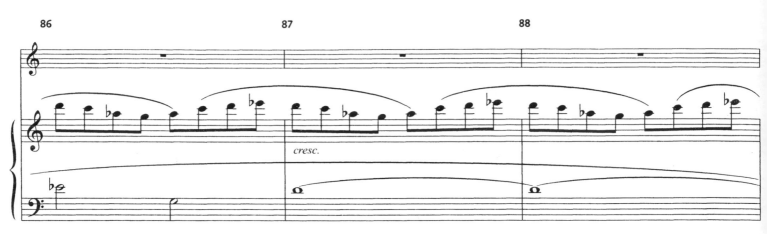

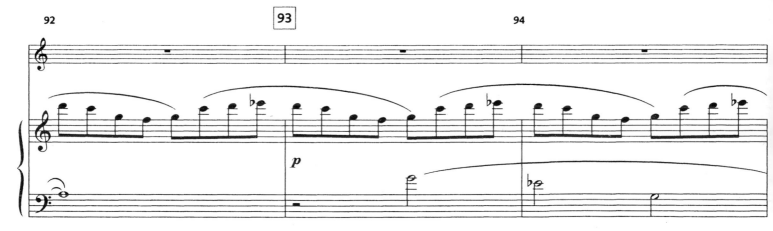

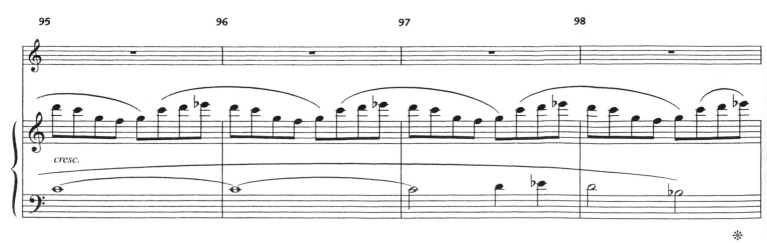

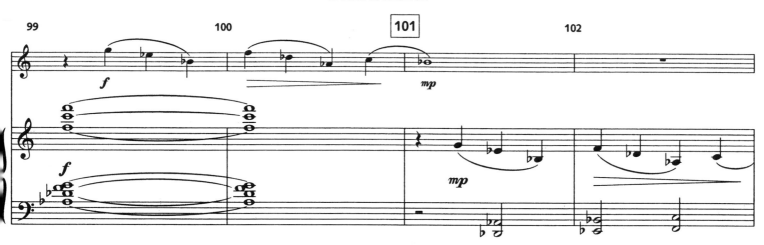

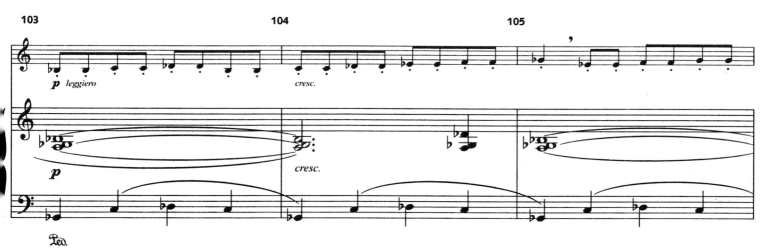

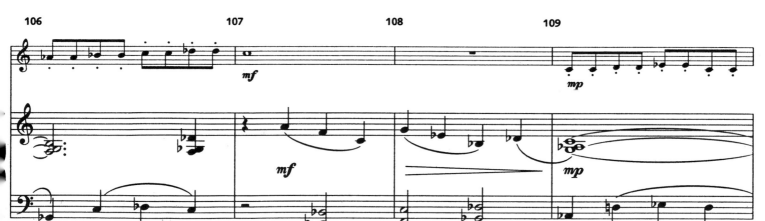

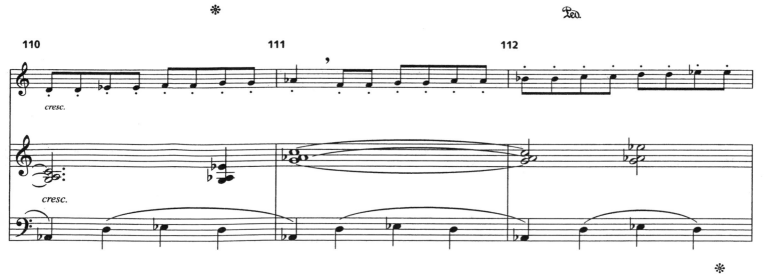

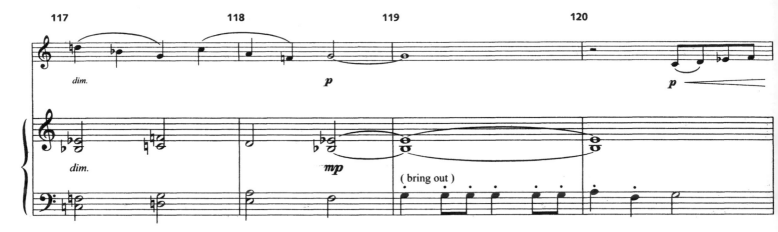

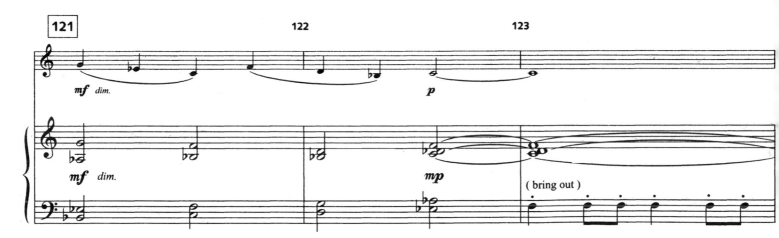

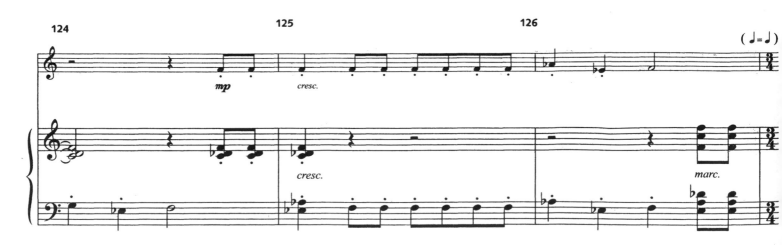

2.

Trumpet in C

Advanced

THREE EPISODES

for Trumpet and Piano

James Curnow

EXCLUSIVELY DISTRIBUTED BY

HAL•LEONARD®
CORPORATION
7777 W. BLUEMOUND RD. P.O. BOX 13819 MILWAUKEE, WI 53213

Commissioned for and first performed by Edward Bach, Trumpet, and Arthur Tollefson, Piano, at the
Focus on Piano Literature, School of Music, The University of North Carolina at Greensboro, June 8 , 2000,
and Second Place Winner of the 2001 International Trumpet Guild Composition Competition.

TRUMPET in C

THREE EPISODES
for Trumpet and Piano

James Curnow (ASCAP)

1.

TRUMPET in C

2.

3.

Trumpet in B♭

Advanced

THREE EPISODES

for Trumpet and Piano

James Curnow

CURNOW® MUSIC

EXCLUSIVELY DISTRIBUTED BY

HAL•LEONARD® CORPORATION

7777 W. BLUEMOUND RD. P.O. BOX 13819 MILWAUKEE, WI 53213

*Commissioned for and first performed by Edward Bach, Trumpet, and Arthur Tollefson, Piano, at the
Focus on Piano Literature, School of Music, The University of North Carolina at Greensboro, June 8 , 2000,
and Second Place Winner of the 2001 International Trumpet Guild Composition Competition.*

TRUMPET in B♭

THREE EPISODES

for Trumpet and Piano

James Curnow (ASCAP)

TRUMPET in B♭

2.

Largo moderato e espressivo (♩. = 48)

mp
sempre legato

Poco accel.

cresc.

17 **Piu mosso** (♩. = 52)

mf   *cresc.*   **ff**

25

dim.   **p**

Poco accel.

mf   *cresc.*

32 **Piu mosso** (♩. = 56)   *Poco accel.*   **Piu mosso** (♩. = 60)

To St. Mute   St. Mute

ff   **p** *slightly detached*

40

f   **p**   **f**   **mp**

3.

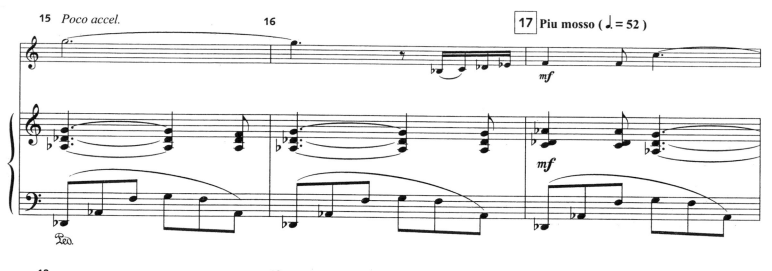

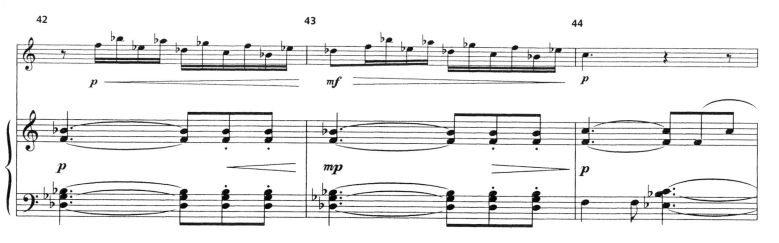

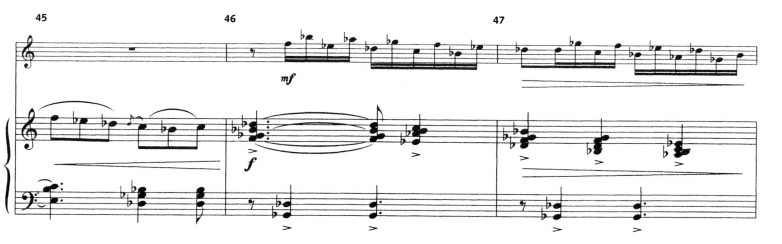

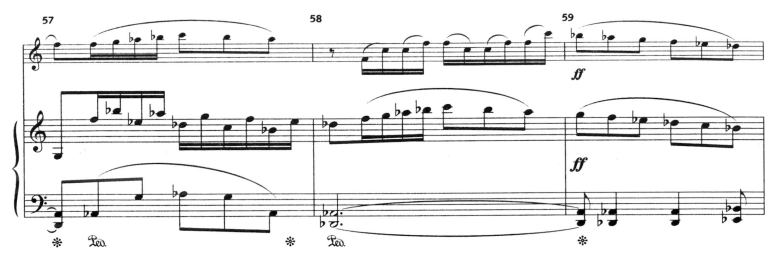

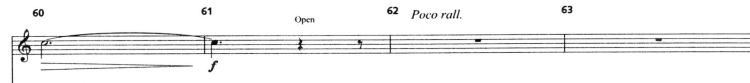

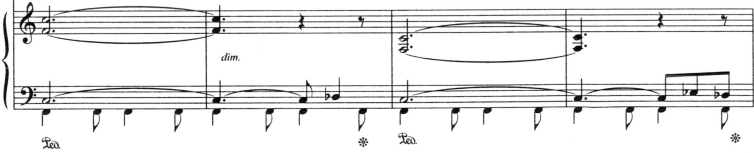

THREE EPISODES

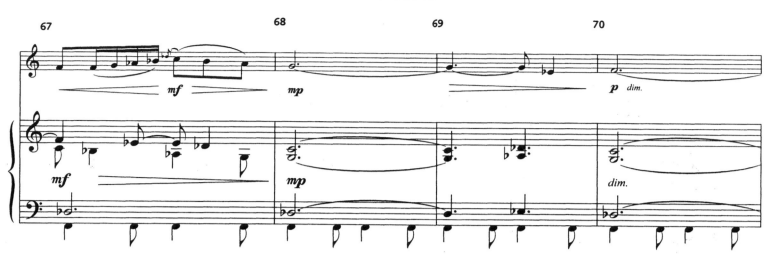

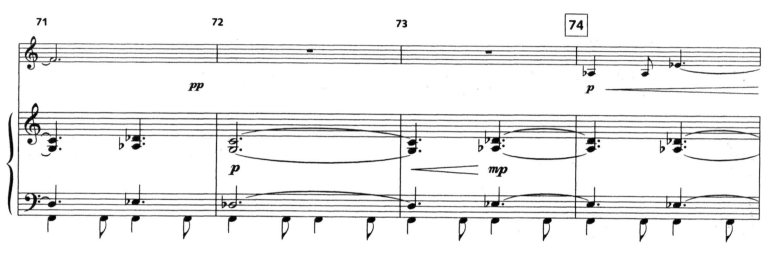

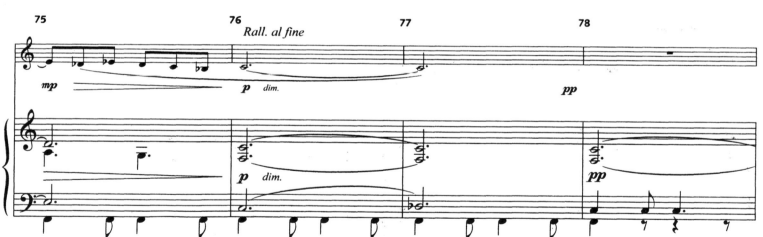

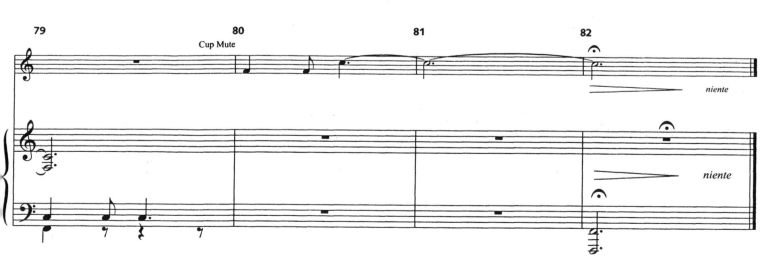

3.

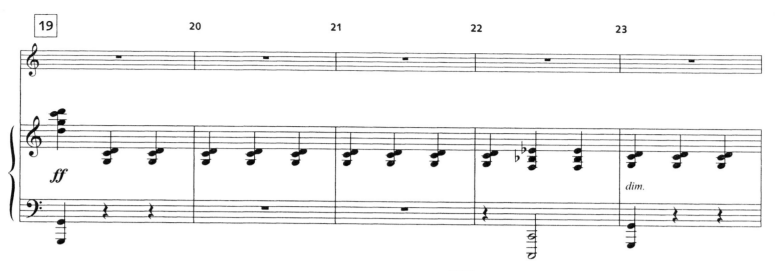

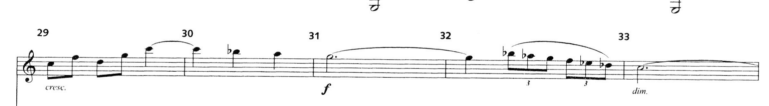

THREE EPISODES

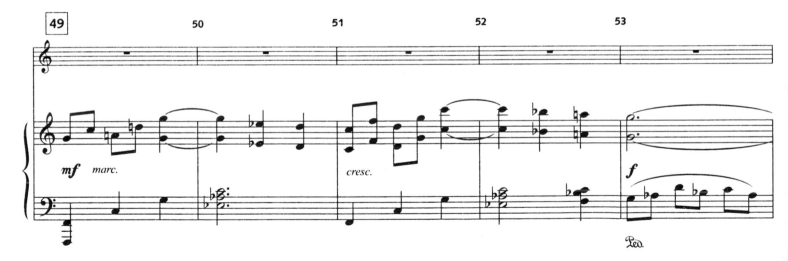

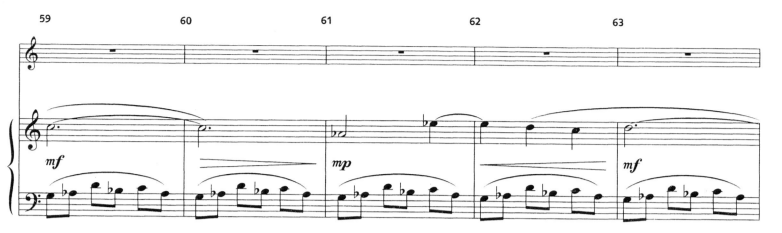

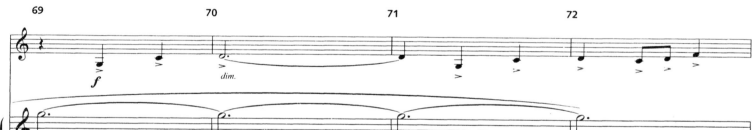

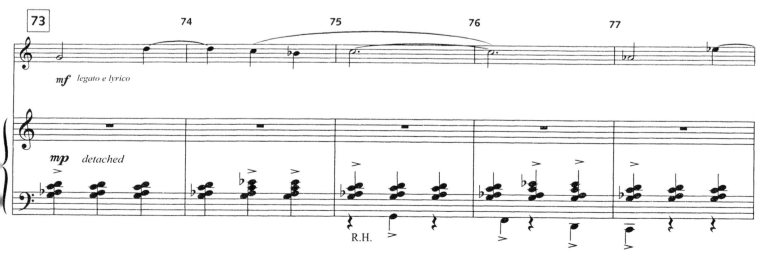

THREE EPISODES

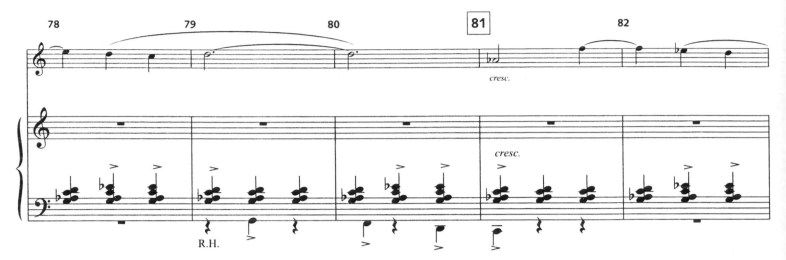

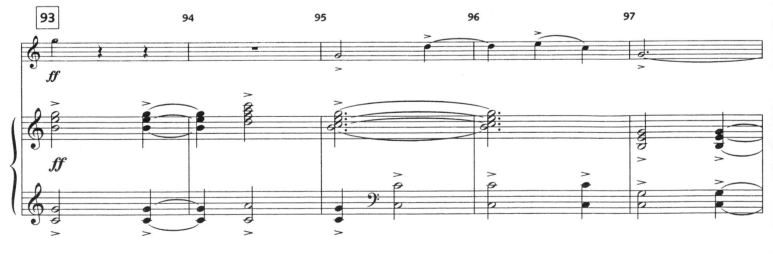

24

26